Science
Grades 6–12

Educational Books 'n' Bingo
EBB5610

English-Language Arts Crossword Puzzles

Grades 6–12

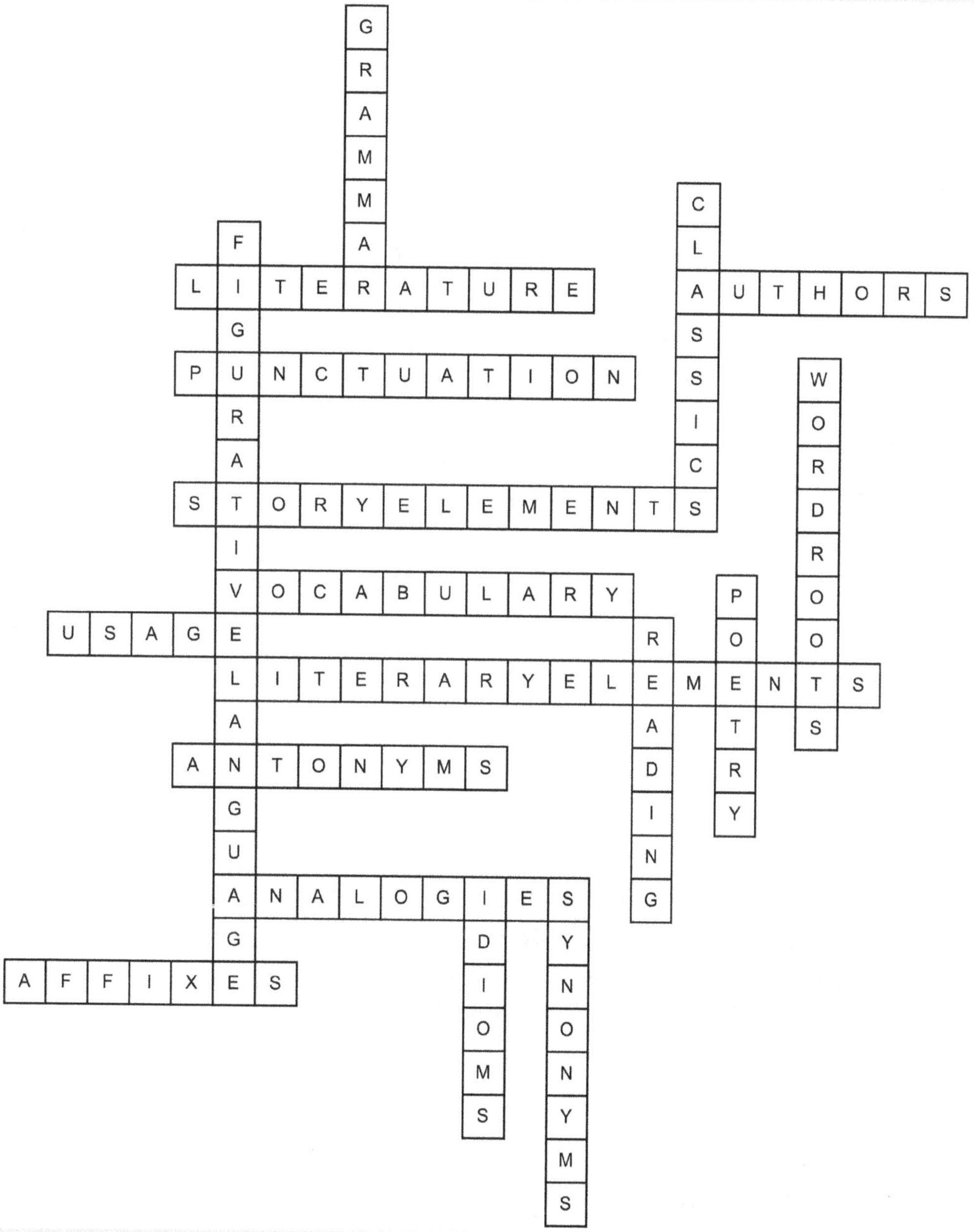
GRAMMAR
CLASSICS
FIGURATIVE LANGUAGE
LITERATURE
AUTHORS
PUNCTUATION
WORD ROOTS
STORY ELEMENTS
VOCABULARY
POETRY
USAGE
READING
LITERARY ELEMENTS
ANTONYMS
ANALOGIES
IDIOMS
SYNONYMS
AFFIXES

Written by Rebecca Stark

ISBN 978-1-56644-561-0

Educational Books 'n' Bingo

Printed in the United States of America.

TABLE OF CONTENTS

*An alphabetical list of answers from which to choose is provided for each crossword puzzle. Use them or not at your discretion.

Grammar and Usage

ACROSS

3. *The* is a definite ___; *a* and *an* are indefinite ones
4. Set of 3 dots used to show that words have been omitted or to create a pause for effect
5. What we do to the first word in a sentence and to proper nouns
6. Unit of grammatical organization that has a subject and predicate
7. Short part of a text that begins a new line and deals with a single idea
8. *Walk, read,* and *think* are ___ verbs
9. Part of a sentence or clause containing a verb and stating something about the subject
10. Ends an interrogatory sentence (2 words)
11. Word or words in which missing letters are replaced by an apostrophe
12. Shortened form of a word
13. Person, place, thing, or idea that is doing or being something
15. Type of sentence that seeks information through a reply
16. Abrupt remark made as an aside or interruption
18. Type of modifying phrase consisting of a preposition and its object
23. Pair of round brackets used to mark off a supplementary word or phrase
26. An oblique stroke in print or writing used between alternatives
27. Identifies whether subject is the speaker, the one spoken to, or the one spoken about
28. Small group of words functioning as a conceptual unit forming component of a clause

DOWN

1. Type of sentence that makes a statement and ends with a full stop
2. Marks used in writing to separate sentences and their elements
4. Used to describe a forceful declarative sentence
10. Set of punctuation marks used to mark beginning and end of a quoted passage (2 words)
14. Punctuation used to join words to indicate that they have a combined meaning
17. *Bookcase*, for example
19. Punctuation mark used in complex lists and when a slight break is preferable to a new sentence
20. Used to indicate possession or omission of letters
21. System and structure of a language
22. Sometimes used to show a range: Example: 147–149 (2 words)
23. Marks the end of a declarative sentence
24. May be used instead of parentheses; larger than en dash (2 words)
25. Set of words that is complete in itself; typically containing a subject and predicate

Grammar and Usage

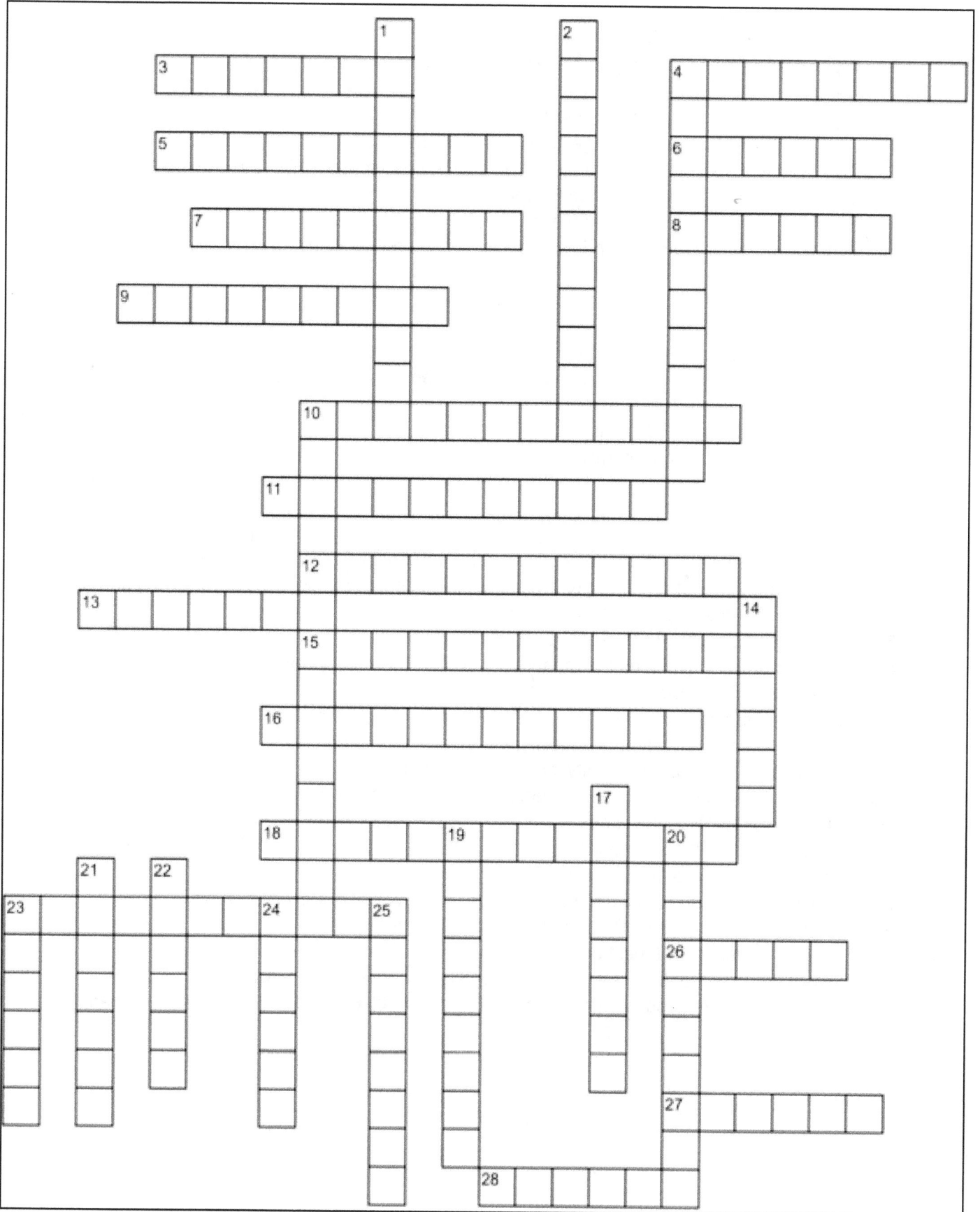

ELA Crossword Puzzles: Gr. 5 & Up

Parts of Speech

ACROSS

3. Type of verb that usually expresses when something occurred
4. Refers to what job the pronoun performs
8. Type of verb that tells what the subject does
9. Word used to modify a verb, adjective, or an adverb
10. Pronouns & adjectives that distinguish the one referred to from others in same class
13. Indicates the person(s) spoken to (2 words)
14. Refers to whether a word is singular or plural
19. Function of the pronoun *him* in this sentence: "The chef broils him a steak."
20. Used to join words, phrases, or clauses.
22. These conjunctions link equal elements
23. Examples: *Oh! Wow!*
24. Name for the characteristic verbs have of expressing time.
25. Noun or pronoun that receives the action of the sentence (2 words)
26. Jennifer : ___ noun :: girl : common noun
27. Indicates the speaker (2 words)
32. Type of verb that tells what the subject is
33. They replace nouns

DOWN

1. Indicates a party other than the speaker or the person spoken
2. Type of pronoun that refers to general persons, places, or things; e.g., *anyone, few* and *many*
4. Noun that denotes a group of individuals
5. Pronoun that shows ownership: e.g., *their* and *her*
6. Word or phrase that makes the meaning of another word or phrase more specific
7. *In, on, above,* and *over*, for example
10. Example: "Hoping to receive extra credit, two extra assignments were done."
11. Type of pronoun that refers to specific person, place, or thing
12. Word used to describe, or modify, noun or a pronoun
15. *The* is a definite one; *a* and *an* are indefinite ones (plural form)
16. Expresses what the subject does or is
17. Names a person, place, or thing
18. Pronouns that may be subjects; e.g., *he, she,* and *I*
21. The words *which* and *what* can serve as ___ adjectives; e.g. Which book did you read?
28. Person, place, or thing performing the action of the sentence
29. Part of a sentence that must contain a verb.
30. Type of pronoun that begins a clause that refers to a noun in a sentence
31. Pronouns used as direct objects, indirect objects, or objects of prepositions; e.g., *him* and *her*

Parts of Speech

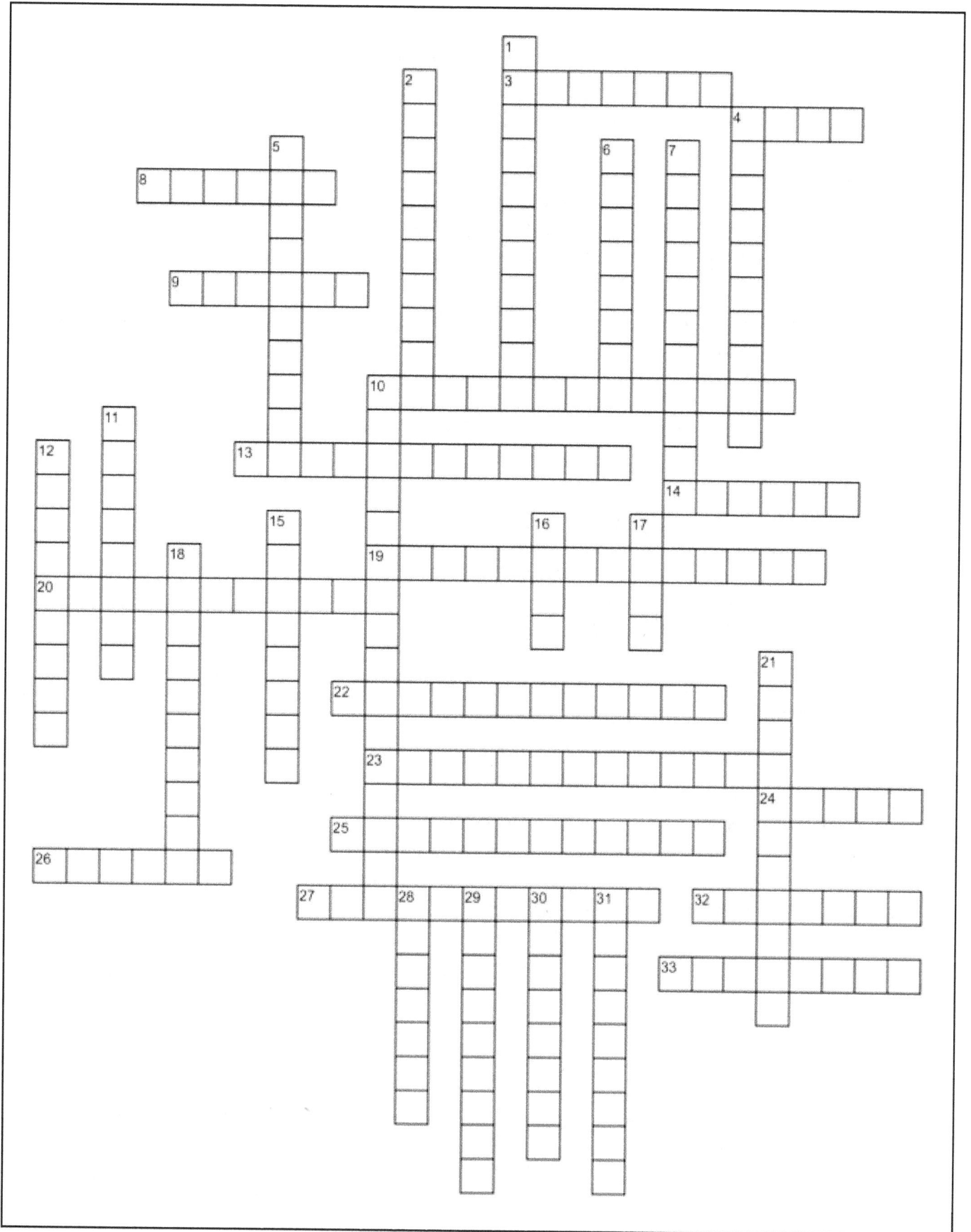

Figurative Language & Other Literary Devices

ACROSS

5. Comparison between two unlike things using the words *like* or *as*
8. Stating of something less strongly than the facts seem to warrant
9. Comparison between two unlike things without the use of *like* or *as*
11. Form of verbal irony in which a person says the opposite of what he or she means
14. Sometimes called blended words; ; e.g., *brunch* and *motel* (2 words)
15. Use of an object, character or idea to represent something else
16. Use of words that sound like the sounds they describe
19. Bestowing of human qualities on inanimate objects, ideas, and animals
20. Repetition of consonant sounds
22. Substitution of one term with another that is associated with that term, such as using "the Crown" to refer to the king
23. Substitution of a less explicit term for an offensive, explicit term
26. Narrative technique that interrupts the chronological sequence of events
27. Language characteristic of a particular region or group
28. Refers to how something is not as it seems

DOWN

1. An exaggeration
2. Spoken words between characters in a literary work
3. Reference in a literary work to something outside of the work
4. Dictionary meaning of a word
6. To drop hints about things that will occur later in the story
7. Portraying of animals or inanimate objects as people
10. "It's not the best movie I ever saw" is an example
12. Figurative language that uses words that sound the same but have different meaning
13. An expression whose meaning cannot be deduced from their literal definitions
17. Overused phrase or expression
18. Associated meaning of a word or a phrase
21. Figure of speech that combines two usually contradictory term
24. Short saying in general use, stating a general truth or piece of advice
25. Use of descriptive language that appeal to the readers' senses

Figurative Language & Other Literary Devices

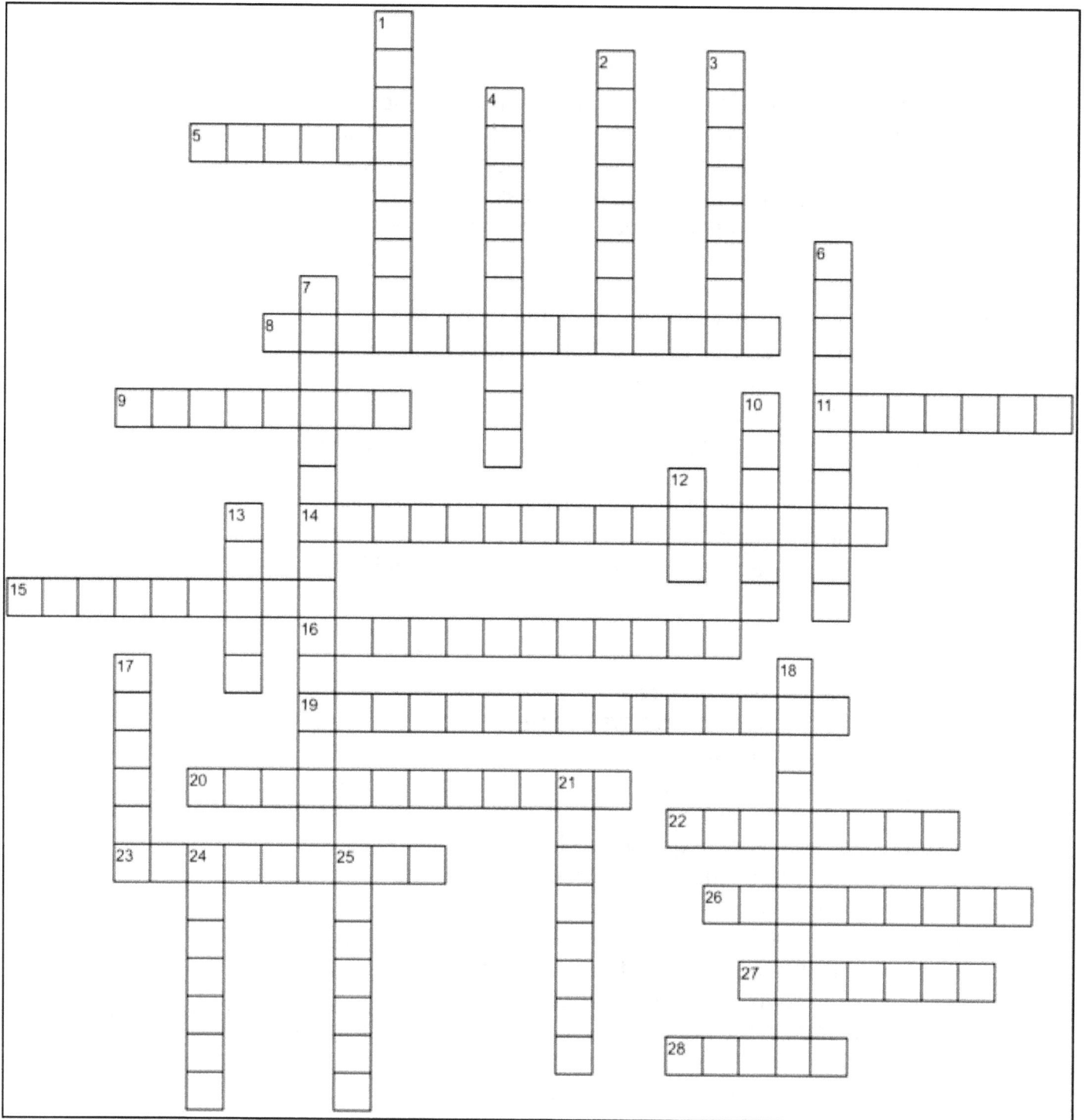

Elements of Literature

ACROSS

5. Major turning point in a story
7. Quality that makes readers wonder what will happen next
8. Literary work designed for performance by actors in a theater; also called a play
9. Time, place, and circumstance in which a story takes place
10. Genre whose imaginary elements are explained by science rather than magic (2 words)
13. Use of an object, character, or idea to represent something else
14. Main character in a literary work
16. Suspenseful situation at end of chapter
17. Struggle that occurs between opposing forces in a plot
18. Short introductory section of a plot that provides background information
20. What happens in denouement of a plot
23. Main character's adversary
24. Author's manner of writing: sentence structure, use of figurative language, tone, etc.
26. Perspective from which a story is told (3 words)
29. Literary work that pokes fun at the weaknesses of a society
30. Writer of a literary work
31. Some positive character ___: kind, loyal, intelligent, and honest

DOWN

1. Author's attitude toward the writing
2. Person in a novel, play, or movie
3. Spoken words between characters in a literary work
4. Main idea of a literary work; e.g., Good v. Evil
6. Language characteristic of a particular region or group
7. Character with traits associated with a particular group of people
11. Method used by author to develop a character
12. Work of prose long enough to be divided into chapters
15. Sequence of causal events in a story
19. Reference in a literary work to something outside of the work
21. Piece of writing at the end of a literary work; antonym of prologue
22. Feeling the author creates for the readers
25. With the addition of the prefix "auto-" it is a story about the author
27. Someone who tells a story
28. Genre that uses magic and supernatural forms

Elements of Literature

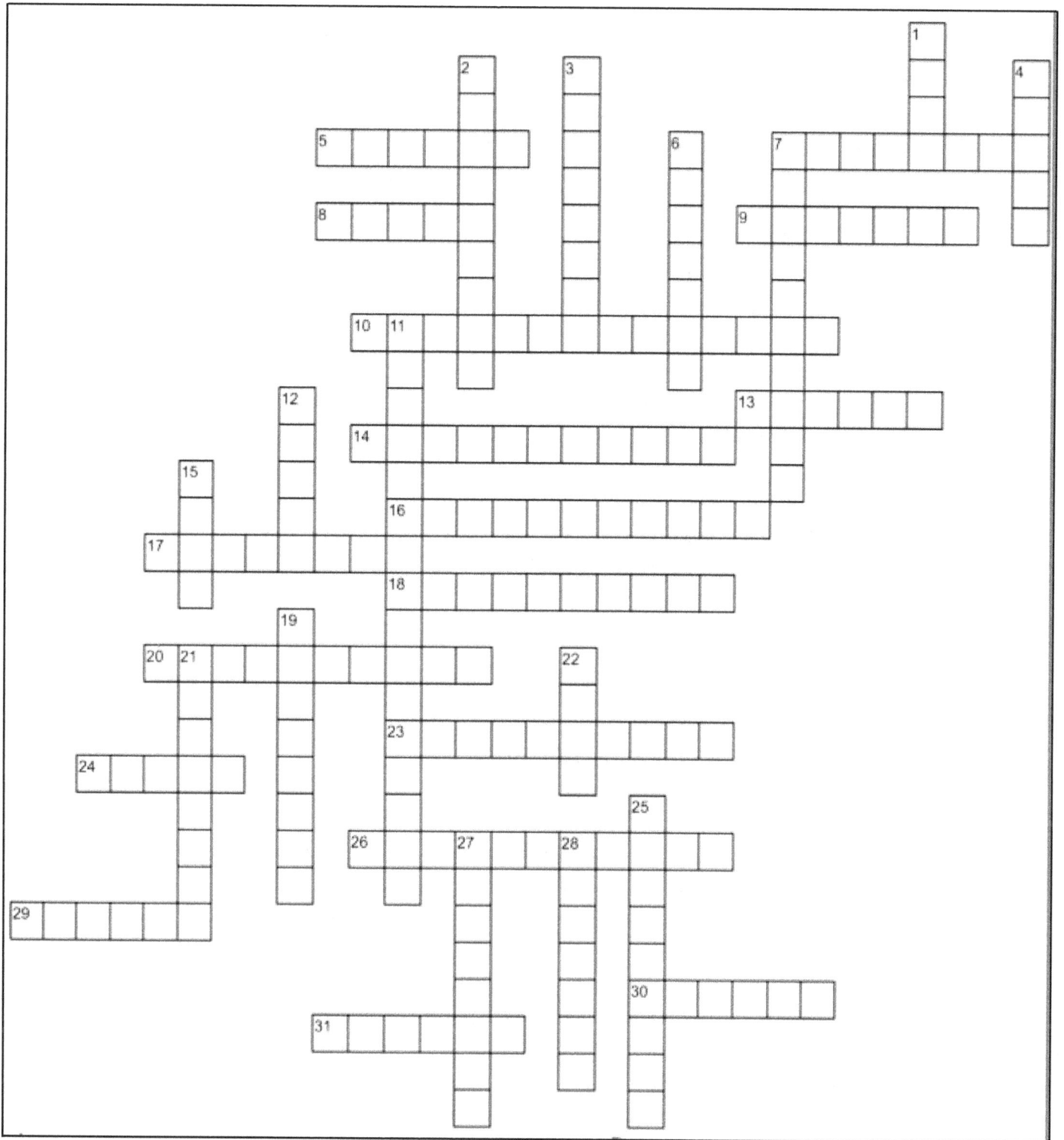

© Barbara M. Peller   ELA Crossword Puzzles: Grades 6 & Up

Poetry

ACROSS

3. Pattern of strong and weak sounds
4. Japanese poem with 5 unrhymed lines
6. Basic rhythmic structure of a verse; defined by the number of feet and the accent pattern
7. Also called a verse; measured by the number of feet
10. Repetition of consonant sounds within words
13. A 19-line poem with two repeating rhymes and two refrains
14. Continuation of a sentence from one line or couplet into the next
15. Examples: iambic, trochaic, anapestic, dactylic and spondaic
16. Prose : paragraph :: poetry : ___
17. Repetition of vowel sounds within non-rhyming words
19. Poetry with the musical quality of a song
23. Use of words that sound like the sounds they describe
26. A 5-line stanza
28. Narrative poetry often set to music
29. Long narrative poem
30. Prose and ___ are major divisions of literature
31. Person who writes poetry
32. A 3-line poem

DOWN

1. Any 4-lined poem or stanza of a poem
2. Humorous 5-line poem with 1 couplet and 1 triplet
5. A 14-line poem written in iambic pentameter
8. Possible ___ schemes for quatrains: *aabb* and *abab*
9. Single metrical line of poetry; sometimes used as synonym for stanza
11. System of marking metrical patterns of a line of poetry
12. Repetition of initial consonant sounds
16. Tanka has 31; haiku has 17
18. Short, humorous, biographical poem
20. Poem with 2 lines that rhyme and have the same meter
21. Short text inscribed on a tombstone
22. Japanese poem with 3 unrhymed lines
24. Type of poem whose first letters of each line usually spell a word or name
25. Long, serious poems that originated with the ancient Greeks
27. Use of descriptive language that appeals to the readers' senses

Poetry

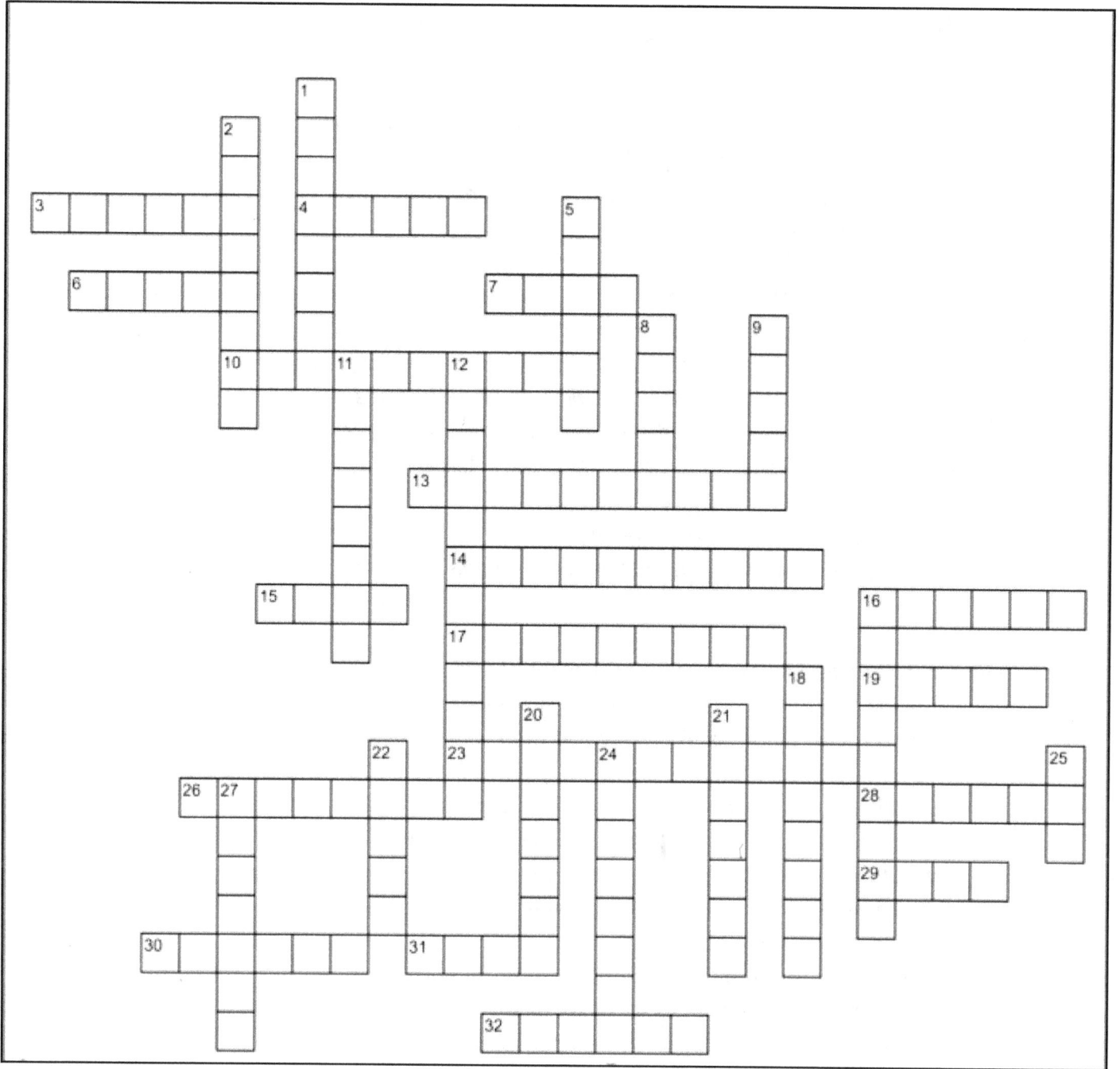

13

Famous Authors and Their Works

ACROSS

2. Best known for picture book *The Very Hungry Caterpillar*
7. Author of *A Wrinkle in Time,* Newbery Medal Winner
8. Author and poet; author of "The Telltale Heart" and other horror stories
9. Winner of Newbery Medal for *Dear Mr. Henshaw*
11. Scottish novelist and poet; author of *Treasure Island* and *The Strange Case of Dr Jekyll and Mr Hyde*
12. Author of *Holes,* Newbery Medal Winner
13. Author/illustrator of *The Polar Express* and *Jumanji:* Chris Van ___
16. Best known for her detective novels, including *Murder on the Orient Express,* and many others
17. British writer famous for *The Wind in the Willows*
19. Danish author best known for "The Ugly Duckling" and other fairy tales
20. British novelist who wrote *The Lion, the Witch and the Wardrobe*
22. Winner of Newbery Medal for *Bridge to Terabithia* and *Jacob Have I Loved*
25. Author of "Rip Van Winkle," "The Legend of Sleepy Hollow," and other short stories
26. Author of *Charlie and the Chocolate Factory*
28. Author of *Tales of a Fourth Grade Nothing*
29. *Sense and Sensibility, Pride and Prejudice,* and *Emma* are among her works

DOWN

1. English author, best known for his books about Winnie the Pooh
3. Author of the Percy Jackson and the Olympians Series
4. Winner of Newbery Medal for *The Giver* and *Number the Stars*
5. Author of classic novel *Little Women*
6. English author of *A Christmas Carol* and other works now considered classics
10. English writer best known for children's books, such as *The Tale of Peter Rabbit*
11. English author whose plays include *Hamlet, Macbeth, Othello,* and many others
14. Created the beloved character Curious George
15. Author of *To Kill a Mockingbird*
17. Author of *Coraline* and *The Graveyard Book*
18. British novelist who created the Harry Potter character
21. Author of popular children's books *Charlotte's Web* and *Stuart Little*
23. Author of *The Hobbit*
24. Best known for her Gothic novel *Frankenstein: or, The Modern Prometheus*
27. Created the characters Tom Sawyer and Huckleberry Finn; Samuel Langhorne Clemens
30. Author/illustrator of *Where the Wild Things Are,* a Caldecott Medal Winner

Famous Authors and Their Works

For each clue, give the last name of the author.

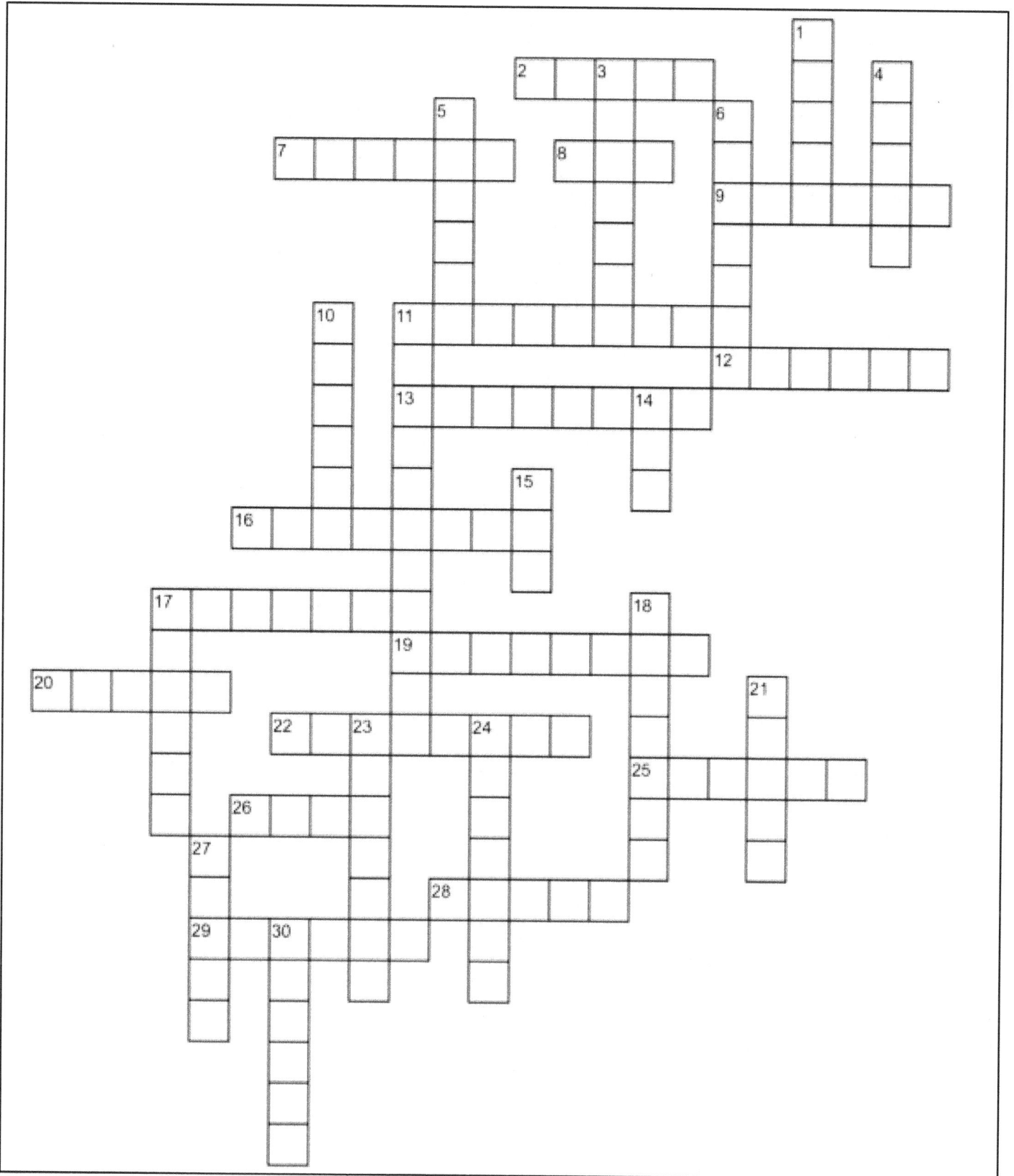

ELA Crossword Puzzles: Grades 6 & Up

Word Roots and Affixes

ACROSS

4. Showing a loss of mental faculties due to old age; based on Latin root meaning "old"
6. Root of word meaning "a large bedroom for several people"
7. Means "friendly"; from Latin word *amicus,* meaning "friend"
8. Placed at the beginning or end of a root, stem, or word or in middle of word to change meaning
10. Affix attached at beginning or end of a word or base to form a new word with a related meaning
11. Arrangement of events in the order of their occurrence; based on Greek root meaning "time"
12. To take in or contain as part of a whole; based on a root that means "body"
13. Affix attached at end of a word or base to form a new word with a related meaning
14. Done without choice; based on the Latin affixes *-vol-*, meaning "wish," and *in-,* meaning "not"
17. Based on Latin root meaning "pleasing" and the prefix meaning "not"
19. Damage that cannot be repaired; Latin root meaning "build" + prefix meaning "removal or reversal"
24. To make clear; based on Latin root meaning "clear" + suffix meaning "to make or to cause to be"
25. Relating to young people; based on Latin root meaning "young"
26. Existing or done alone; based on Latin root *solus*
28. A basic word to which affixes are added
29. Latin affix meaning "good or well"
30. Period of ten years; based on Greek root meaning "ten"
32. Ability to understand and share the feelings of another; based on Greek root meaning "feeling"
34. Suffix added to *defend* to get a word meaning "one accused in a court of law"

DOWN

1. Lasting for only a limited period of time; based on Latin root meaning "time"
2. Work that continues the story of an earlier one; has same Latin root as the word *consequence*
3. Add a prefix meaning "not" to a word with a Latin root meaning "death" to get this word meaning "never dying"
5. Greek suffix meaning "pain"
7. Antibody that counteracts a poison; root meaning "poison" + prefix meaning "against"
9. Used to describe angry and bitter speech; based on Greek root *acri-,* meaning "bitter"
15. Aggressive; warlike; based on Latin root meaning "war"
16. Latin root meaning "hand or weigh"; root of *pendant* and *suspense*
18. Not able to be conquered; based on Latin root meaning "conquer" and prefix meaning "not"
20. Optical instrument used for viewing far away objects; based on roots meaning "far" and "see"
21. Latin root meaning "speak" + prefix meaning "against"
22. Not believable; combines prefix meaning "not" and root meaning "believe"
23. Latin root meaning "use" or "take"; found in word meaning "to eat, drink, or ingest"
27. Along with *tact* and *tag,* this affix means "touch"
31. Words built upon this root involve a killing
33. Optical instrument used for viewing very small objects; based on roots meaning "small" and "see"

Word Roots and Affixes

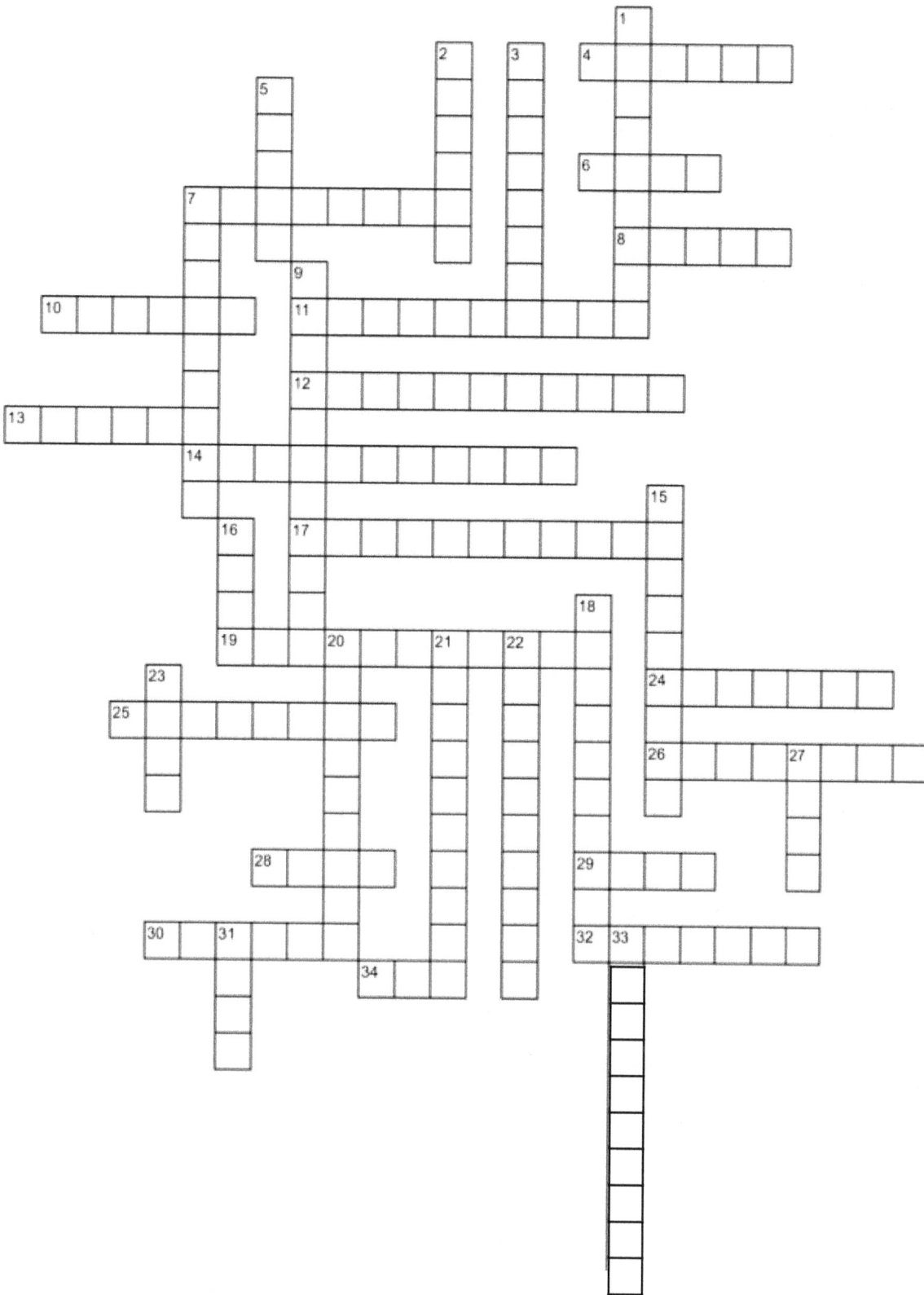

Vocabulary

ACROSS

3. to grimace involuntarily
5. frank
7. a distant view along an opening
9. without suffering any injury
10. something that causes pain and suffering
13. to imply
14. prolonged quarrel or dispute
17. failing to achieve the desired results
18. characteristic of a mother
19. disheartened
15. the great size or extent of something
20. to desire or yearn for
21. a revolutionary
26. mysterious, especially in an unsettling way
27. with reckless haste

ACROSS

1. a sudden impulsive idea or action
2. skill or expertise in a particular activity
4. to captivate
5. a victim in a war or accident
6. seriousness
8. to strengthen
10. to accept the truth of something
11. dishonest
12. to challenge; to face up to and deal with a difficult situation
15. the great size or extent of something
16. a ruckus
22. to beseech or beg
23. to present an honor or gift
24. a domicile
25. submissive
28. depressing to consider; gloomy

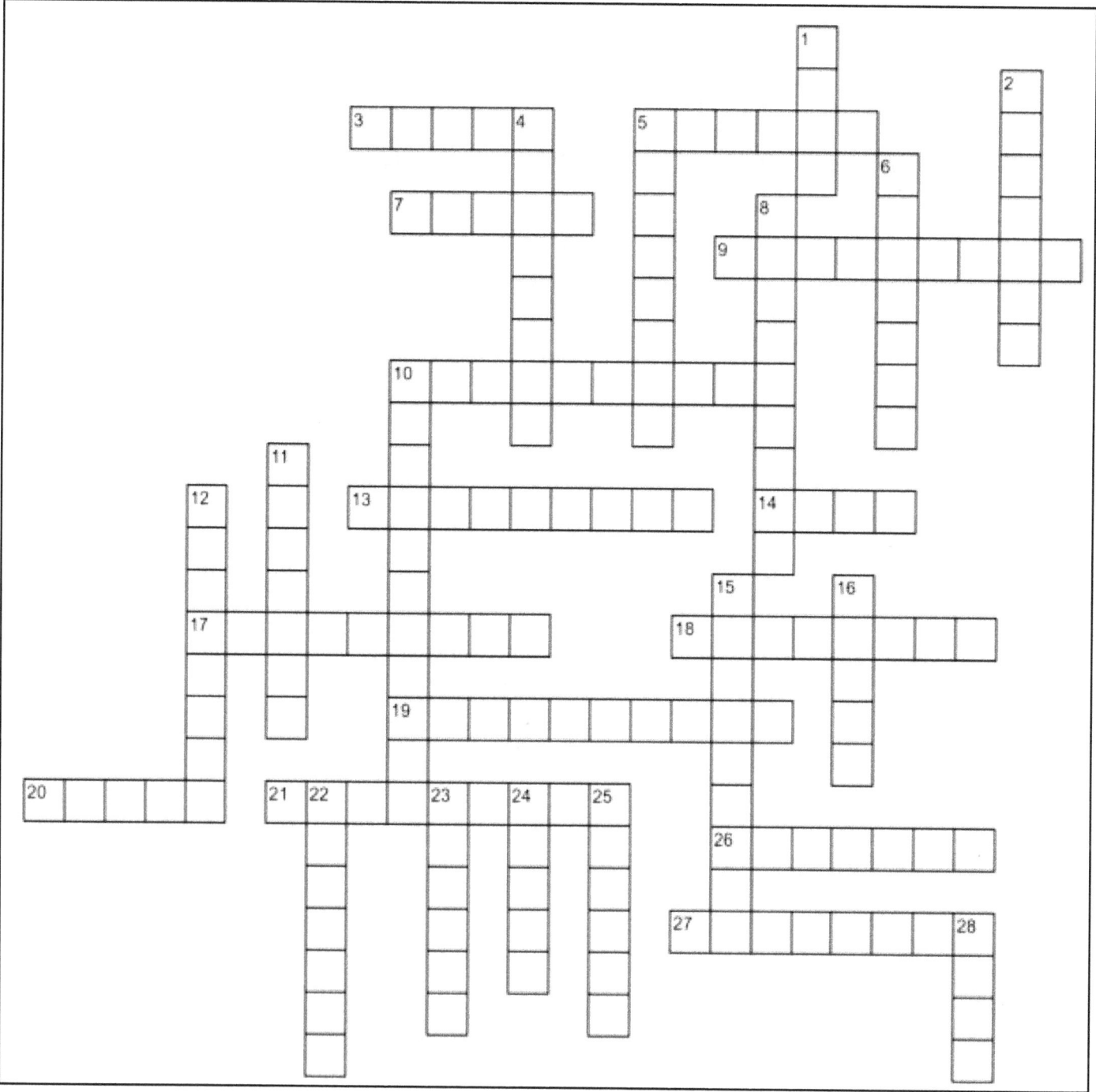

Vocabulary

More Vocabulary

ACROSS

2. showing caution about possible dangers
4. extreme anger
6. to roar, especially in pain or anger
7. to climb or move in an awkward way
8. most extreme; greatest
10. to give satisfaction
12. a defect or imperfection
14. according to the usual practices
15. deliberately cruel or violent
16. to cause someone to become confused
17. dreary
18. a spoken or written account
20. to survey goods for sale in a leisurely and casual way
22. deeply upset and agitated
25. to break or burst suddenly
26. enthusiastic and public praise
27. wandering
31. a thing that exists only in one's imagination

DOWN

1. to gradually wear away
3. poisonous
5. lack of interest and enthusiasm
6. a person who boasts about achievement
9. to overturn in the water
11. to flood; to overwhelm
12. to astonish
13. unwilling; reluctant
19. so delicate as to be difficult to analyze or describe
21. gloomy; sulky
23. to rebuke or admonish
24. causing repulsion or horror
28. having a strong and unpleasant taste or smell
29. a dog is one
30. agile
32. amusement; merriment

More Vocabulary

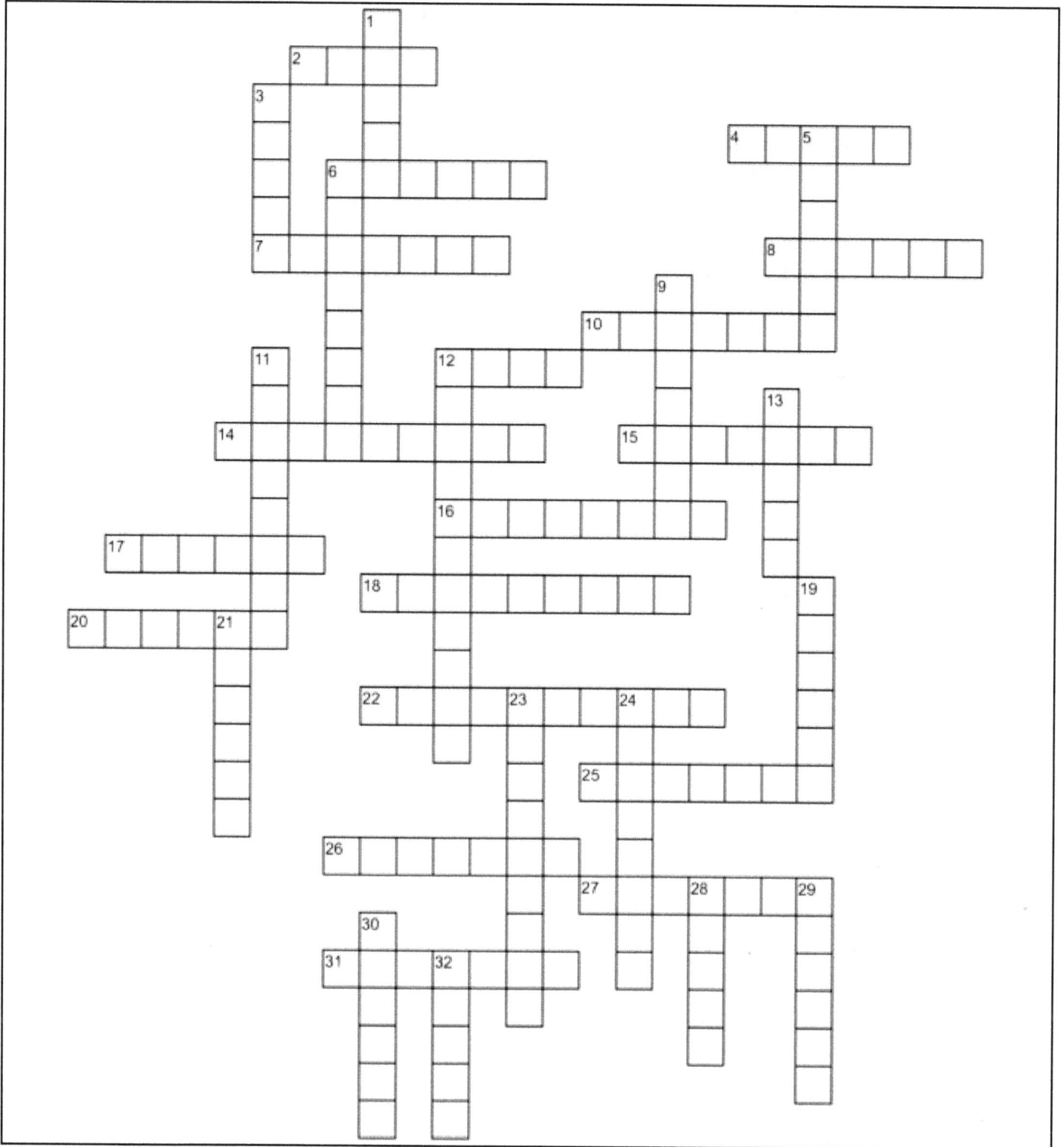

ELA Crossword Puzzles: Grades 6 & Up

Synonyms and Antonyms

ACROSS

4. Synonym of *avoid*
6. Synonym of *perceptive*
7. Synonym of *befuddle*
8. Antonym of *respectable*
10. Synonym of *subside*
13. Synonym of *drip*
14. Antonym of *predictable*
15. Synonym of *embarrass*
17. Synonym of *joyous*
18. Synonym of *quicken*
20. Antonym of *illegal*
23. Antonym of *inconspicuous*
24. Synonym of *alienate*
27. Synonym of *vigorous*
28. Synonym of *pursue*
29. Synonym of *fatal*
30. Synonym of *comprehend*
31. Synonym of *contemplate*
32. Synonym of *ostentatious*
33. Antonym of *finale*
34. Antonym of *tolerant*
35. Antonym of *disagree*

DOWN

1. Antonym of *assist*
2. Antonym of *immaculate*
3. Synonym of *beg*
5. Synonym of *vengeful*
9. Antonym of *unmemorable*
11. Synonym of *rouse*
12. Antonym of *inconsequential*
16. Synonym of *defect*
19. Synonym of *agitated*
21. Synonym of *egregious*
22. Antonym of *careful*
25. Synonym of *genuine*
26. Antonym of *delight*
31. Antonym of *cowardice*

Synonyms and Antonyms

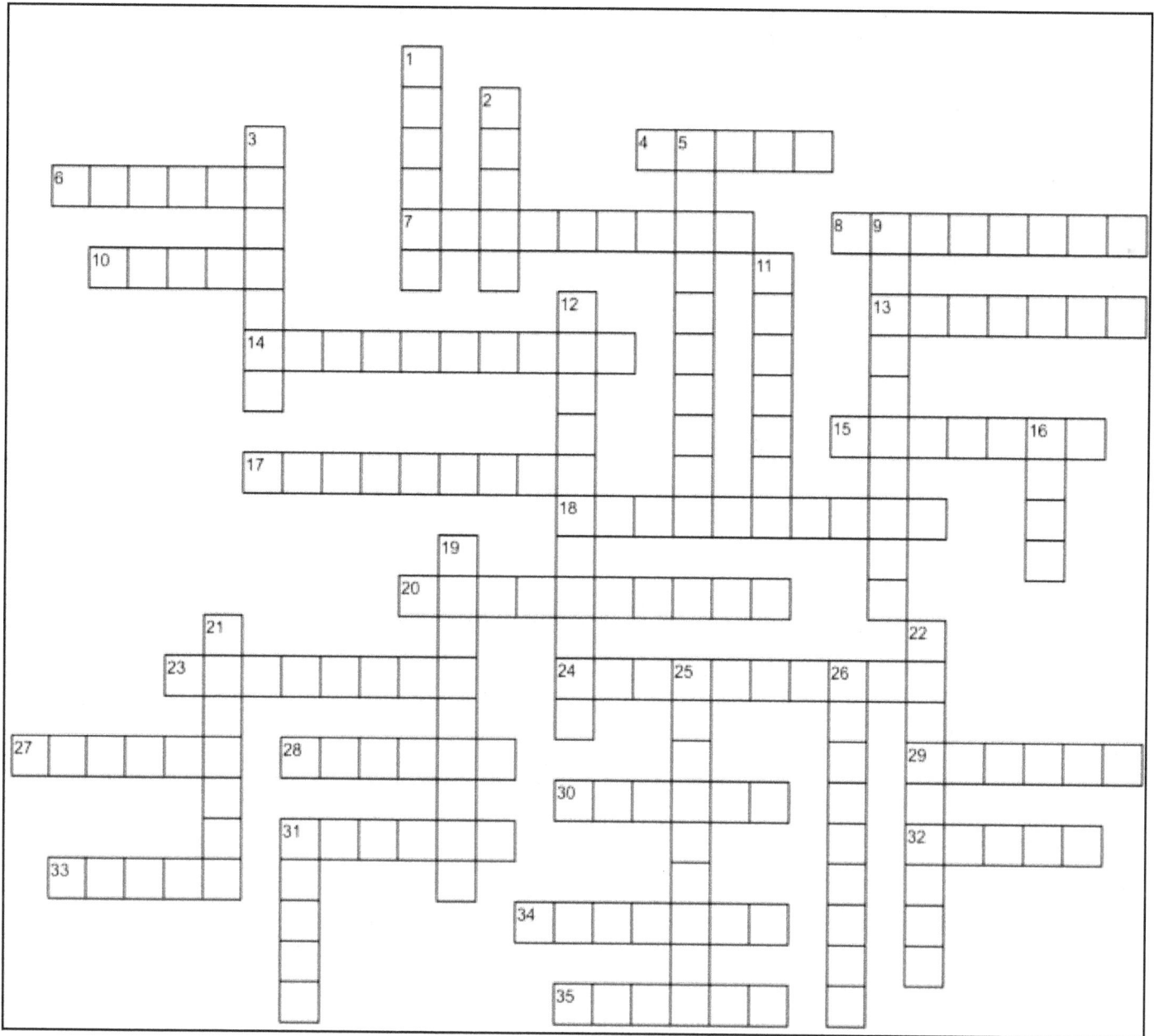

ELA Crossword Puzzles: Grades 6 & Up

Classic & Modern Authors Word Search

```
J  V  T  M  Y  E  R  S  A  D  A  H  L  L  K  N
J  Q  W  E  C  R  X  H  H  G  E  E  R  H  O  L
U  T  A  P  K  C  E  B  N  I  E  T  S  S  O  P
S  E  I  T  S  I  T  R  U  C  B  H  N  W  N  K
T  E  N  N  T  U  Q  E  P  A  T  E  R  S  O  N
E  R  R  R  A  I  N  W  Z  F  V  Y  O  D  Q  G
R  Z  E  A  O  R  B  Z  U  E  C  E  T  P  E  Z
L  G  C  M  E  H  R  B  T  R  O  W  L  I  N  G
O  N  G  V  O  P  T  S  A  A  H  S  S  Y  I  N
N  I  L  I  X  H  S  W  L  B  L  A  D  L  O  N
D  L  N  L  Q  N  G  E  A  L  C  C  L  X  E  D
O  P  R  O  E  N  Q  S  K  H  E  E  O  I  U  E
N  I  C  K  I  D  I  O  A  A  N  N  K  T  B  M
Z  K  C  V  J  W  O  R  E  I  H  L  G  A  T  U
G  I  R  A  E  G  B  V  P  N  O  S  U  L  O  L
D  I  G  L  R  B  I  S  A  T  M  M  B  U  E  B
```

Search for these authors: up, down or diagonal.

ALCOTT	BABBITT	BAUM
BLUME	CURTIS	DAHL
DICKENS	DOYLE	HAWTHORNE
HOMER	IRVING	JUSTER
KIPLING	L'ENGLE	LEWIS
LONDON	LOWRY	MYERS
O'DELL	PATERSON	POE
SPINELLI	STEINBECK	STEVENSON
TOLKIEN	TWAIN	VERNE

Literary Genres Word Search

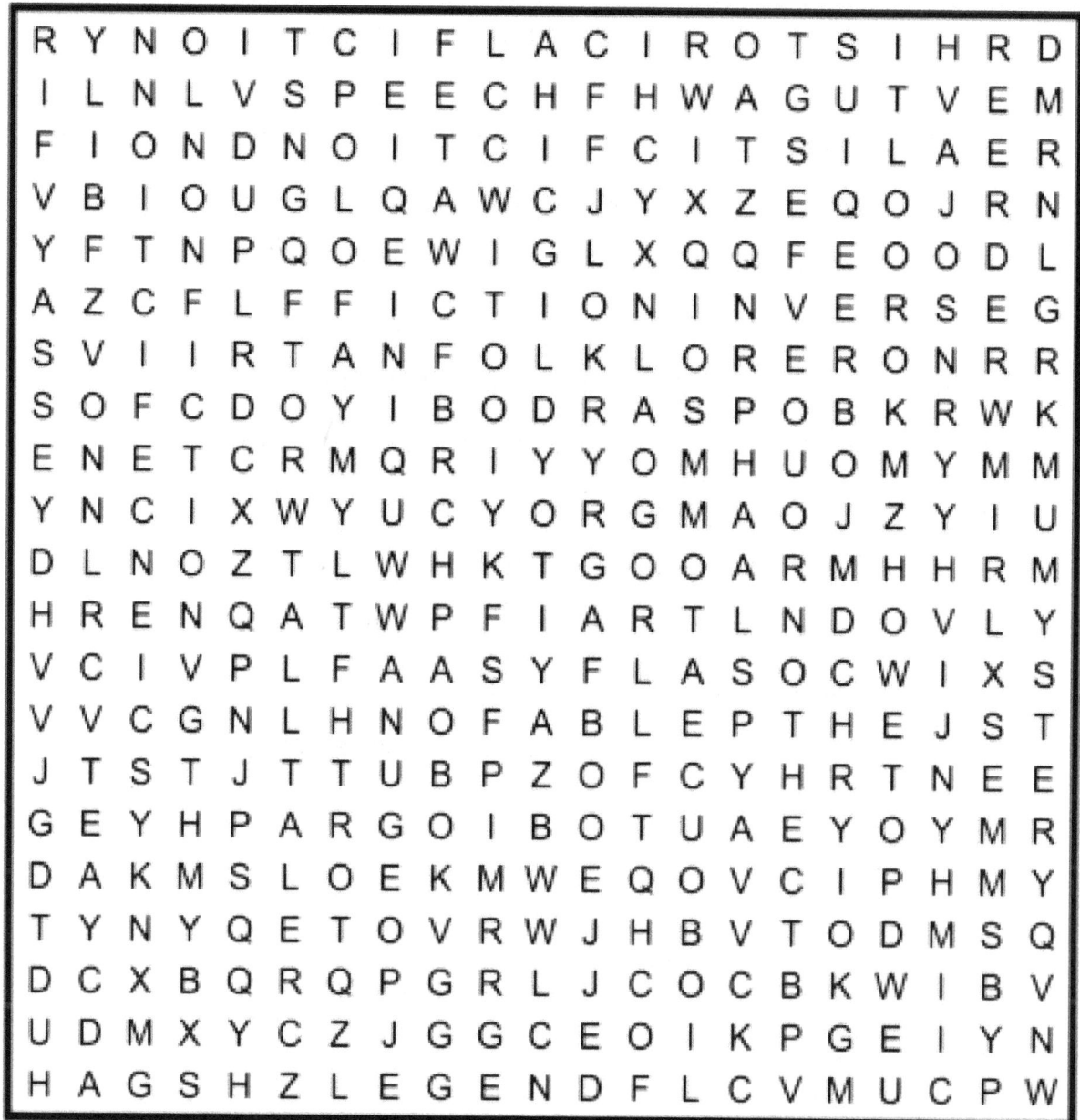

```
R Y N O I T C I F L A C I R O T S I H R D
I L N L V S P E E C H F H W A G U T V E M
F I O N D N O I T C I F C I T S I L A E R
V B I O U G L Q A W C J Y X Z E Q O J R N
Y F T N P Q O E W I G L X Q Q F E O O D L
A Z C F L F F I C T I O N I N V E R S E G
S V I I R T A N F O L K L O R E O N R R
S O F C D O Y I B O D R A S P O B K R W K
E N E T C R M Q R I Y Y O M H U O M Y M M
Y N C I X W Y U C Y O R G M A O J Z Y I U
D L N O Z T L W H K T G O O A R M H H R M
H R E N Q A T W P F I A R T L N D O V L Y
V C I V P L F A A S Y F L A S O C W I X S
V V C G N L H N O F A B L E P T H E J S T
J T S T J T T U B P Z O F C Y H R T N E E
G E Y H P A R G O I B O T U A E Y O Y M R
D A K M S L O E K M W E Q O V C I P H M Y
T Y N Y Q E T O V R W J H B V T O D M S Q
D C X B Q R Q P G R L J C O C B K W I B V
U D M X Y C Z J G G C E O I K P G E I Y N
H A G S H Z L E G E N D F L C V M U C P W
```

Search for these literary genres: up, down or diagonal.

AUTOBIOGRAPHY	BIOGRAPHY	DRAMA
ESSAY	FABLE	FAIRY TALE
FANTASY	FICTION	FICTION IN VERSE
FOLKLORE	HISTORICAL FICTION	HORROR
HUMOR	LEGEND	MYSTERY
MYTHOLOGY	NONFICTION	POETRY
REALISTIC FICTION	ROMANCE	SCIENCE FICTION
SHORT STORY	SPEECH	TALL TALE

ELA Crossword Puzzles: Grades 6 & Up

Hidden Anagrams

Find the anagrams hiding in each sentence.

1. The guide told us to be silent and to listen carefully for the sound of a whip-poor-will.

2. My sister Sophie cannot resist a sale on shoes!

3. I was about to rinse my hair when I heard a siren outside my window.

4. The math teacher suspected that there was a cheater in the class.

5. The senator believed that the man on trial was guilty of treason.

6. Zack is the nicest boy in the school. He wouldn't even harm an insect!

7. Mom is in the kitchen waiting for the sauce to thicken.

8. Rebecca complained that her meat was tough, so Emma said she ought to send it back.

9. My brother laughed when I tried to row the canoe in the ocean.

10. Jake squirted lemon on his honeydew melon.

11. Tokyo is the capital city of Japan. Kyoto used to be its capital.

12. I expect my friend to come over after school except if she has a test tomorrow.

13. The club's president said he would veto the proposal even if the members vote to pass it.

14. The arrogant chef was annoyed when Dad said there was too much tarragon in the stew.

15. The student claimed that there was a medical reason that he was absent for the test.

Solutions*

*Optional Lists of Answers

Alphabetical lists of the answers are provided. These may be used to help solve the puzzle from the beginning, to assist those having difficulty, or not at all.

Grammar and Usage

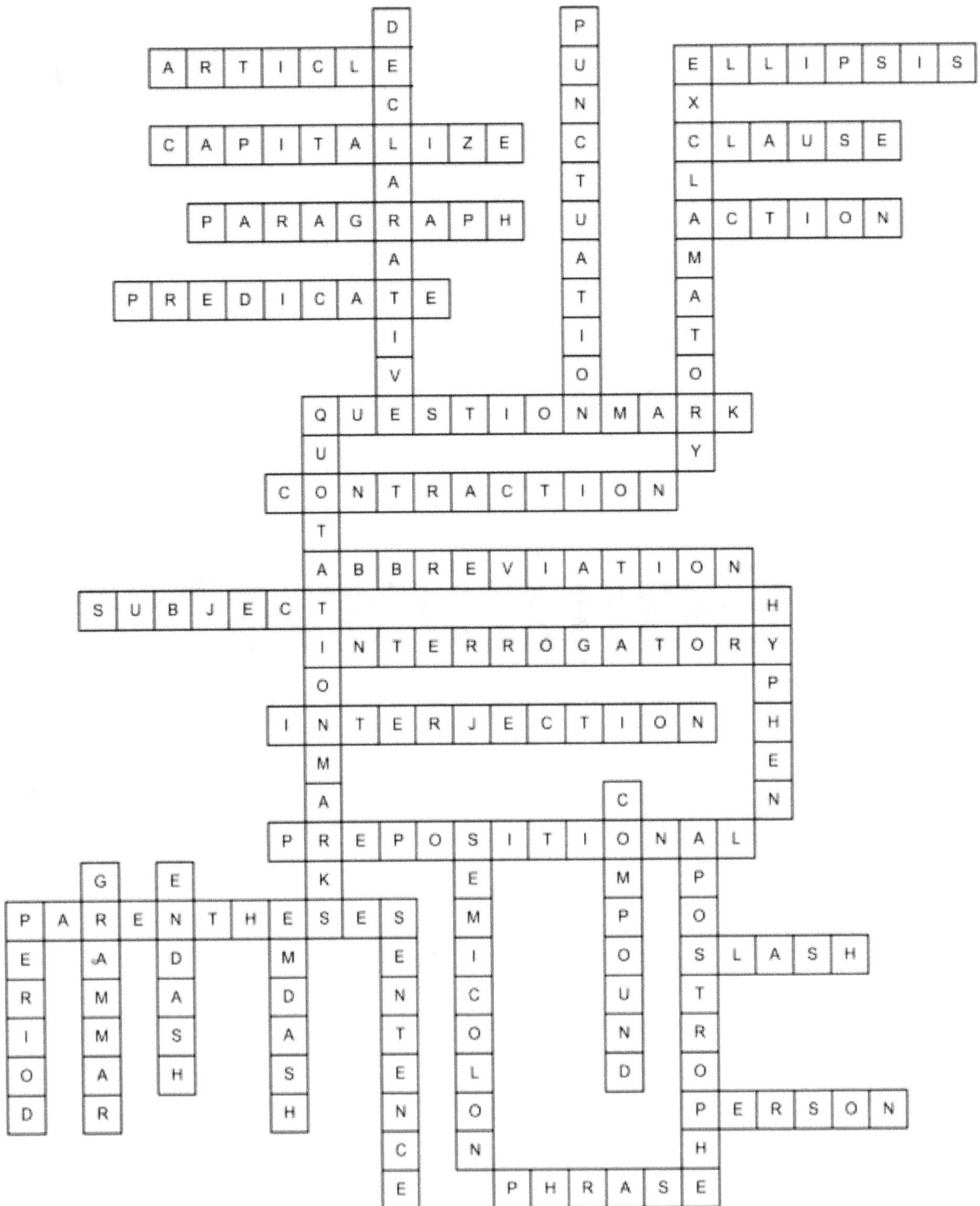

ARTICLE
CAPITALIZE
PARAGRAPH
PREDICATE
ELLIPSIS
CLAUSE
ACTION
QUESTION MARK
CONTRACTION
ABBREVIATION
SUBJECT
INTERROGATORY
INTERJECTION
PREPOSITIONAL
PARENTHESES
SLASH
PERSON
PHRASE

DECLARATIVE
PUNCTUATION
EXCLAMATORY
QUOTATION MARK
INTONATION
PERIOD
GRAMMAR
EM DASH
EN DASH
SEMICOLON
SENTENCE
COMPOUND
APOSTROPHE
HYPHEN

Parts of Speech

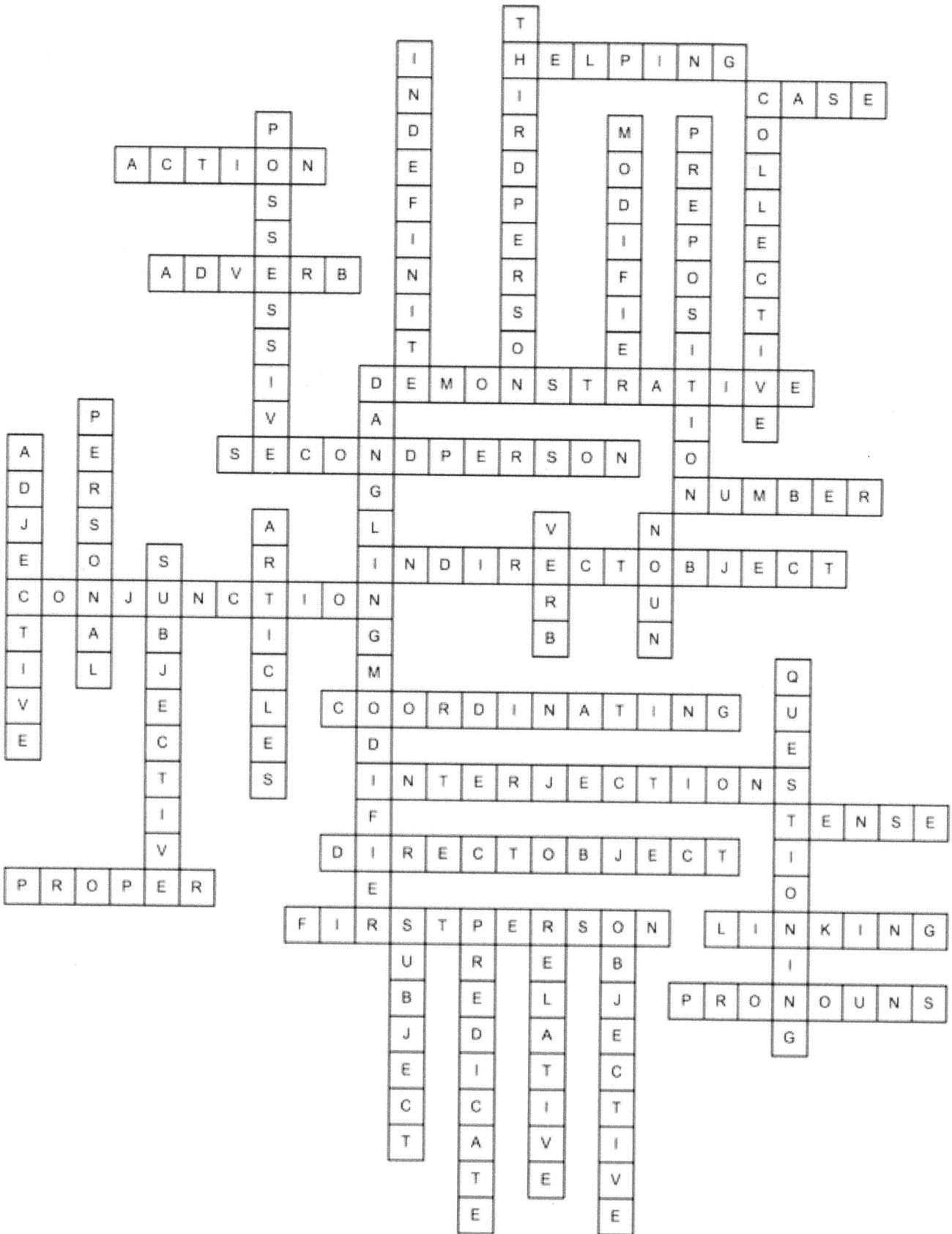

A crossword puzzle with the following words:

Across:
- HELPING
- CASE
- ACTION
- ADVERB
- DEMONSTRATIVE
- SECOND PERSON
- NUMBER
- INDIRECT OBJECT
- CONJUNCTION
- COORDINATING
- INTERJECTIONS
- TENSE
- DIRECT OBJECT
- PROPER
- FIRST PERSON
- LINKING
- PRONOUNS

Down:
- THIRD PERSON
- INDEFINITE
- MODIFIES
- PREPOSITION
- COLLECTIVE
- POSSESSIVE
- DANGLING
- PERSONAL
- ADJECTIVE
- ADVERB
- SUBJECTIVE
- ARTICLES
- NUMBER
- VERB
- NOUN
- ADJECTIVE
- QUESTIONING
- SUBJECT
- PREDICATE
- RELATIVE
- OBJECTIVE

Figurative Language & Other Literary Devices

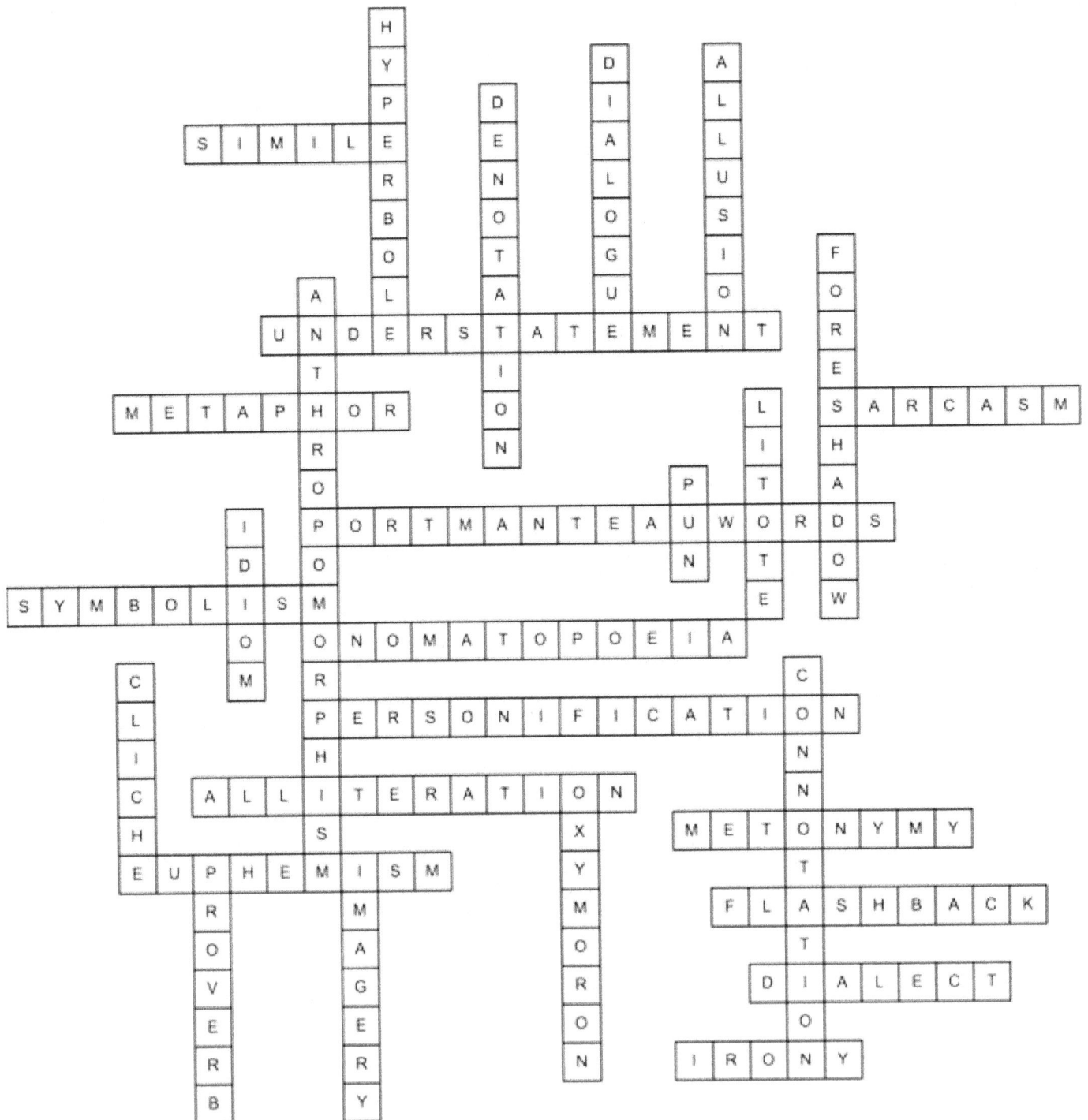

SIMILE

UNDERSTATEMENT

METAPHOR

SARCASM

PORTMANTEAUWORDS

SYMBOLISM

ONOMATOPOEIA

PERSONIFICATION

ALLITERATION

METONYMY

EUPHEMISM

FLASHBACK

DIALECT

IRONY

Down words (letters visible):
HYPERBOLE
DENOTATION
DIALOGUE
ALLUSION
FORESHADOW
ATTRIBUTE
HROMR / METAPHOR
LITERATES
PUNTE
IDIOM
CLICHE
PHS
PROVERB
IMAGERY
OXYMORON
CONNOTATION
CONTEXT

Elements of Literature

Poetry

A completed crossword puzzle with the following answers:

- RHYTHM
- METER
- LIMERICK
- QUATRAIN
- TANKA
- CONSONANCE
- SCANSION
- VILLANELLE
- LINE
- SONNET
- RHYME
- VERSE
- ENJAMBMENT
- NARRATIVE
- FOOT
- ASSONANCE
- STANZA
- LYRIC
- ONOMATOPOEIA
- HAIKU
- COUPLET
- CONCRETE
- METAPHOR
- CLICHE
- SYLLABLE
- BALLAD
- CINQUAIN
- IMAGERY
- POETRY
- POET
- TERCET
- EPIC
- ODE

Famous Authors and Their Works

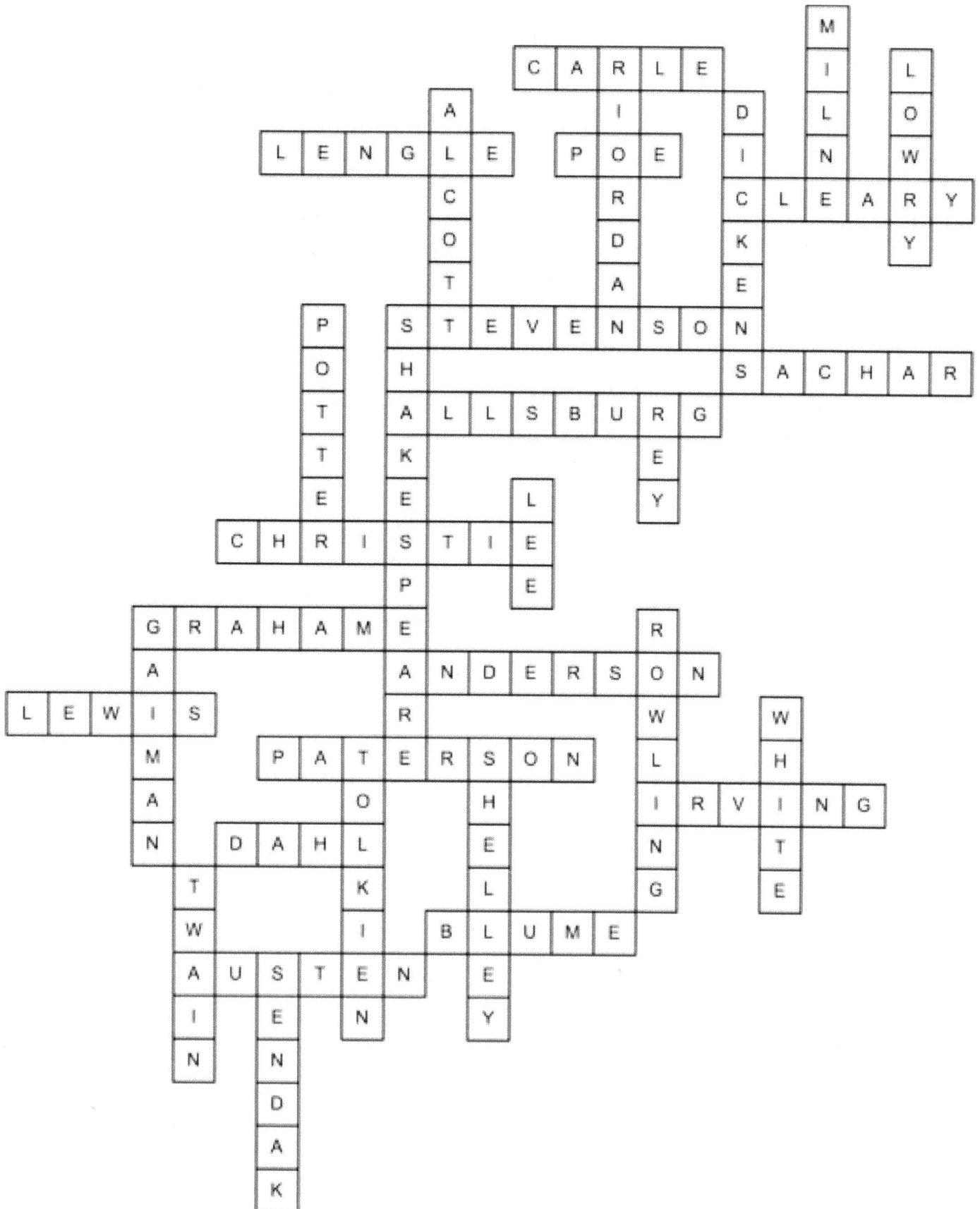

CARLE

MILNE

LOWRY

LENGLE   POE   DINKCLEARY

ALCOTT

RIORDAN

STEVENSON   SACHAR

POTTEE   SHALLSBURG   CHRISTIE   LEE   GRAHAME   ANDERSON   ROWLING   LEWIS   PATERSON   IRVING   DAHL   BLUME   TWAIN   AUSTEN   SENDAK   WHITE

Word Roots and Affixes

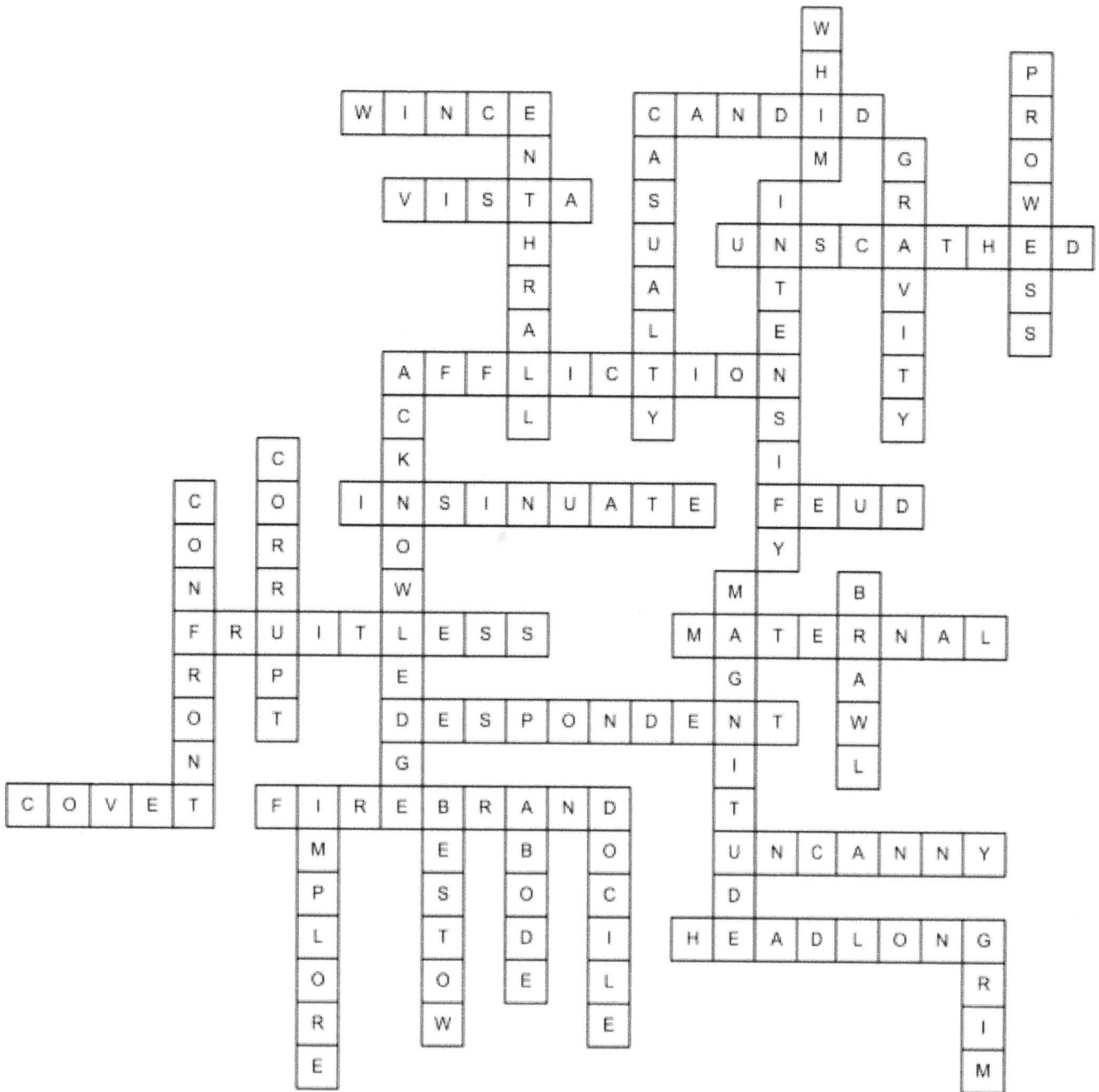

Vocabulary

W I N C E

C A N D I D

V I S T A

U N S C A T H E D

A F F L I C T I O N

I N S I N U A T E

F E U D

F R U I T L E S S

M A T E R N A L

D E S P O N D E N T

C O V E T

F I R E B R A N D

U N C A N N Y

H E A D L O N G

More Vocabulary

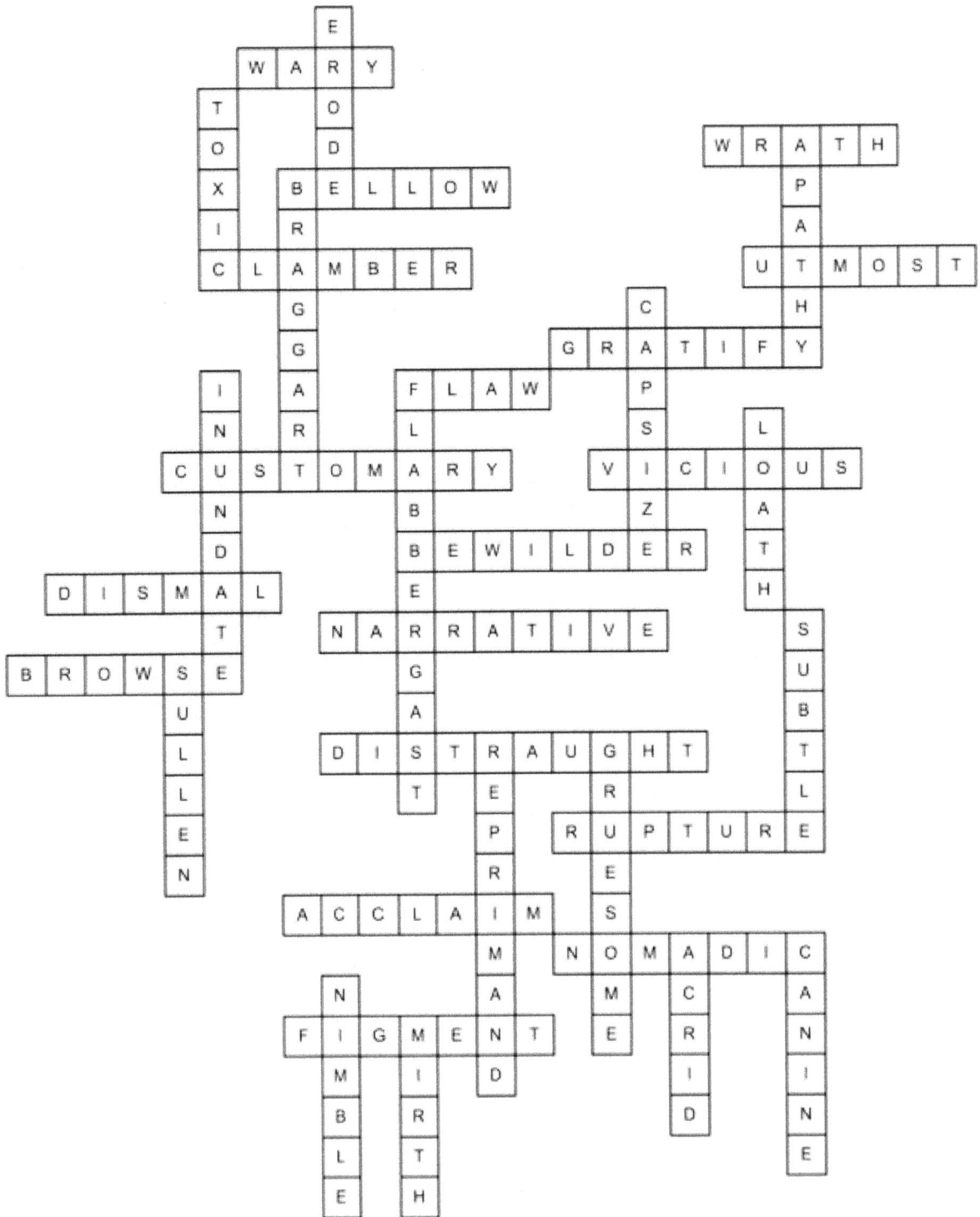

The completed crossword grid contains the following words:

- WARY
- EODD (E, O, D, D — down from top)
- TOXIC
- BELLOW
- CLAMBER
- WRATH
- UPATH / PATH
- UTMOST
- GRATIFY
- FLAW
- GRATIFY
- CUSTOMARY
- VICIOUS
- INN / INNUNDATE
- DISMAL
- BEWILDER
- NARRATIVE
- BROWSE
- SULLEN
- DISTRAUGHT
- RUPTURE
- ACCLAIM
- NOMADIC
- FIGMENT
- CANINE
- SUBTLE
- LOATH
- PERPRESS
- CAPSIZE

© Barbara M. Peller   36   ELA Crossword Puzzles: Grades 6 & Up

Synonyms and Antonyms

ASTUTE

ABATE

DUMBFOUND

AVERT

INFAMOUS

TRICKLE

CAPRICIOUS

MORTIFY

EXUBERANT

ACCELERATE

LEGITIMATE

ANTAGONIZE

FLAGRANT

ROBUST   ASPIRE   LETHAL

FATHOM   GAUDY

PONDER

DEBUT

BIGOTED

CONCUR

Down words (visible letters):
IMPEDE, BESEECH, GRIMY, SUBSTS, DISCTIVITV, AGITATA, FORTREWEHYY, PLRTURBD, ANTAGONIZE, BLATAN, LUCK, CONFIGURATE, LINGENT, HEEN

Famous Authors Word Search

```
      1  2  3  4  5  6  7  8  9  10 11 12 13 14 15 16
 1    J  V  T  M  Y  E  R  S  A  D  A  H  L  L  K  N
 2    J  Q  W  E  C  R  X  H  H  G  E  E  R  H  O  L
 3    U  T  A  P  K  C  E  B  N  I  E  T  S  S  O  P
 4    S  E  I  T  S  I  T  R  U  C  B  H  N  W  N  K
 5    T  E  N  N  T  U  Q  E  P  A  T  E  R  S  O  N
 6    E  R  R  R  A  I  N  W  Z  F  V  Y  O  D  Q  G
 7    R  Z  E  A  O  R  B  Z  U  E  C  E  T  P  E  Z
 8    L  G  C  M  E  H  R  B  T  R  O  W  L  I  N  G
 9    O  N  G  V  O  P  T  S  A  A  H  S  S  Y  I  N
10    N  I  L  I  X  H  S  W  L  B  L  A  D  L  O  N
11    D  L  N  L  Q  N  G  E  A  L  C  C  L  X  E  D
12    O  P  R  O  E  N  Q  S  K  H  E  E  O  I  U  E
13    N  I  C  K  I  D  I  O  A  A  N  N  K  T  B  M
14    Z  K  C  V  J  W  O  R  E  I  H  L  G  A  T  U
15    G  I  R  A  E  G  B  V  P  N  O  S  U  L  O  L
16    D  I  G  L  R  B  I  S  A  T  M  M  B  U  E  B
```

The words below are listed with their starting row and column.

ALCOTT 9:10	BABBITT 10:10	BAUM 13:15
BLUME 16:16	CURTIS 4:10	DAHL 1:10
DICKENS 16:1	DOYLE 11:16	HAWTHORNE 12:10
HOMER 10:6	IRVING 16:2	JUSTER 2:1
KIPLING 14:2	L'ENGLE 11:10	LEWIS 16:4
LONDON 8:1	LOWRY 2:16	MYERS 1:4
O'DELL 14:7	PATERSON 5:9	POE 7:14
ROWLING 8:10	SACHAR 9:13	SHAKESPEARE 15:12
SPINELLI 16:8	STEINBECK 3:13	STEVENSON 9:8
TOLKIEN 16:10	TWAIN 1:3	VERNE 9:4

Literary Genres Word Search

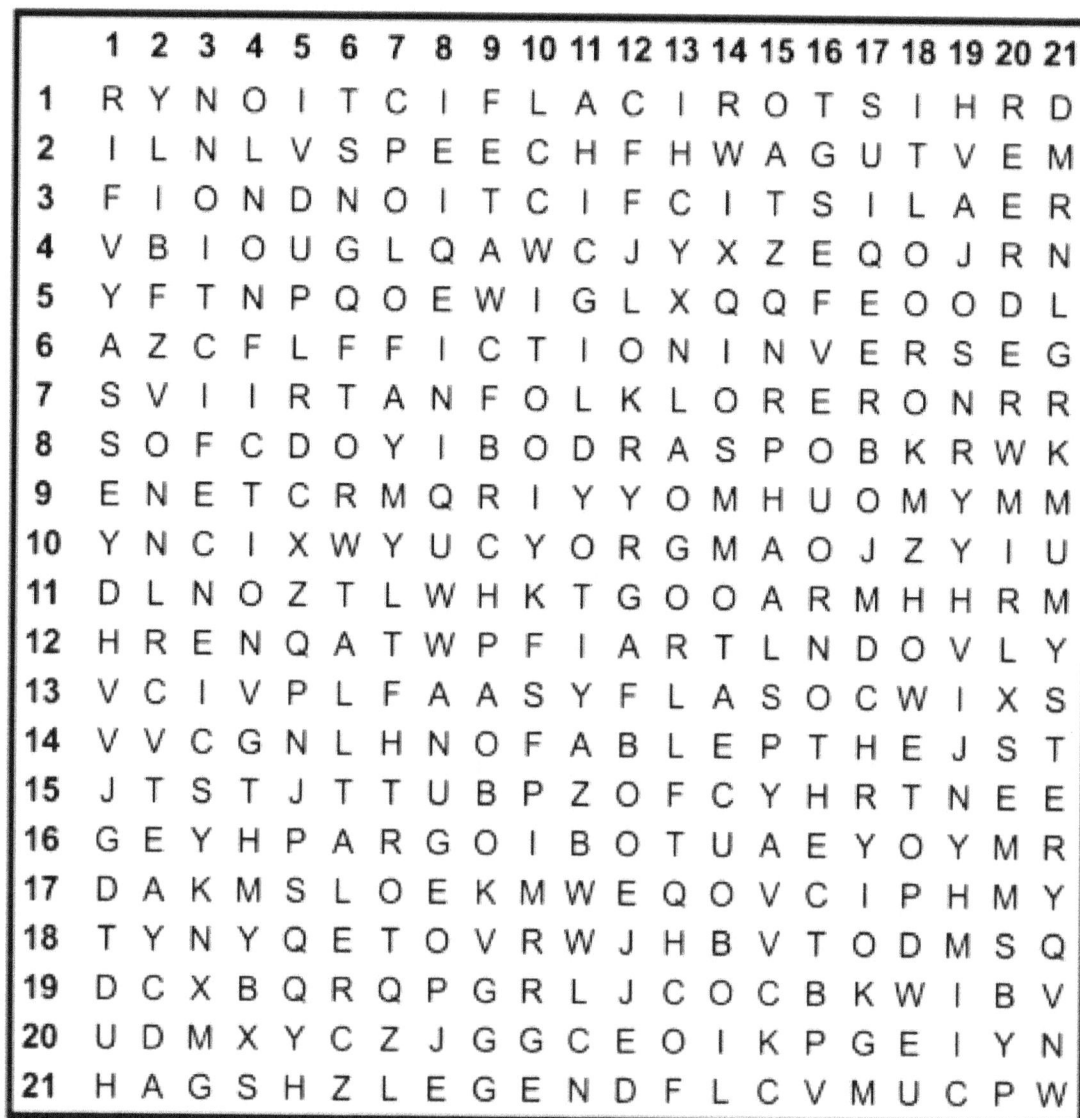

	1	2	3	4	5	6	7	8	9	10	11	12	13	14	15	16	17	18	19	20	21
1	R	Y	N	O	I	T	C	I	F	L	A	C	I	R	O	T	S	I	H	R	D
2	I	L	N	L	V	S	P	E	E	C	H	F	H	W	A	G	U	T	V	E	M
3	F	I	O	N	D	N	O	I	T	C	I	F	C	I	T	S	I	L	A	E	R
4	V	B	I	O	U	G	L	Q	A	W	C	J	Y	X	Z	E	Q	O	J	R	N
5	Y	F	T	N	P	Q	O	E	W	I	G	L	X	Q	Q	F	E	O	O	D	L
6	A	Z	C	F	L	F	F	I	C	T	I	O	N	I	N	V	E	R	S	E	G
7	S	V	I	I	R	T	A	N	F	O	L	K	L	O	R	E	R	O	N	R	R
8	S	O	F	C	D	O	Y	I	B	O	D	R	A	S	P	O	B	K	R	W	K
9	E	N	E	T	C	R	M	Q	R	I	Y	Y	O	M	H	U	O	M	Y	M	M
10	Y	N	C	I	X	W	Y	U	C	Y	O	R	G	M	A	O	J	Z	Y	I	U
11	D	L	N	O	Z	T	L	W	H	K	T	G	O	O	A	R	M	H	H	R	M
12	H	R	E	N	Q	A	T	W	P	F	I	A	R	T	L	N	D	O	V	L	Y
13	V	C	I	V	P	L	F	A	A	S	Y	F	L	A	S	O	C	W	I	X	S
14	V	V	C	G	N	L	H	N	O	F	A	B	L	E	P	T	H	E	J	S	T
15	J	T	S	T	J	T	U	B	P	Z	O	F	C	Y	H	R	T	N	E	E
16	G	E	Y	H	P	A	R	G	O	I	B	O	T	U	A	E	Y	O	Y	M	R
17	D	A	K	M	S	L	O	E	K	M	W	E	Q	O	V	C	I	P	H	M	Y
18	T	Y	N	Y	Q	E	T	O	V	R	W	J	H	B	V	T	O	D	M	S	Q
19	D	C	X	B	Q	R	Q	P	G	R	L	J	C	O	C	B	K	W	I	B	V
20	U	D	M	X	Y	C	Z	J	G	G	C	E	O	I	K	P	G	E	I	Y	N
21	H	A	G	S	H	Z	L	E	G	E	N	D	F	L	C	V	M	U	C	P	W

The words below are listed with their starting row and column.

AUTOBIOGRAPHY 16:15

ESSAY 9:1

FANTASY 12:10

FOLKLORE 7:9

HUMOR 11:9

MYTHOLOGY 17:20

REALISTIC FICTION 3:21

SHORT STORY 18:20

BIOGRAPHY 8:9

FABLE 14:10

FICTION 21:13

HISTORICAL FICTION 1:19

LEGEND 21:7

NONFICTION 3:4

ROMANCE 8:12

SPEECH 2:6

DRAMA 12:17

FAIRY TALE 6:6

FICTION IN VERSE 6:7

HORROR 9:15

MYSTERY 11:21

POETRY 15:10

SCIENCE FICTION 15:3

TALL TALE 11:6

Hidden Anagrams

The anagrams in each sentence are in bold.

1. The guide told us to be **silent** and to **listen** carefully for the sound of a whip-poor-will.

2. My **sister** Sophie cannot **resist** a sale on shoes!

3. I was about to **rinse** my hair when I heard a **siren** outside my window.

4. The math **teacher** suspected that there was a **cheater** in the class.

5. The **senator** believed that the man on trial was guilty of **treason.**

6. Zack is the **nicest** boy in the school. He wouldn't even harm an **insect!**

7. Mom is in the **kitchen** waiting for the sauce to **thicken.**

8. Rebecca complained that her meat was **tough,** so Emma said she **ought** to send it back.

9. My brother laughed when I tried to row the **canoe** in the **ocean.**

10. Jake squirted **lemon** on his honeydew **melon.**

11. **Tokyo** is the capital city of Japan. **Kyoto** used to be its capital.

12. I **expect** my friend to come over after school **except** if she has a test tomorrow.

13. The club's president said he would **veto** the proposal even if the members **vote** to pass it.

14. The **arrogant** chef was annoyed when Dad said there was too much **tarragon** in the stew.

15. The student **claimed** that there was a **medical** reason that he was absent for the test.

Optional Lists of Words and Terms

These lists are provided for your convenience. If a puzzle is used as an introduction or just for fun, you might want to provide the list of words. On the other hand, if the puzzle is being done in lieu of a quiz, you might choose not to utilize them. In either case, solutions to the puzzles are provided.

Grammar and Usage

abbreviation   action   apostrophe   articles   capitalize   clause   compound   contraction   declarative   ellipsis   em dash   en dash   exclamatory   grammar   hyphen   interjection   interrogatory   paragraph   parentheses   period   person   phrase   predicate   prepositional   punctuation   question mark   quotation marks   semicolon   sentence   subject   slash

---

Parts of Speech

action   adjective   adverb   articles   case   collective   conjunction   coordinating   dangling modifier   demonstrative   direct object   first person   helping   indefinite   indirect object   interjections   linking   modifier   noun   number   objective   person   personal   possessive   predicate   preposition   pronouns   proper   questioning   relative   second person   subject   subjective   tense   third person   verb

---

Figurative Language & Other Literary Devices

alliteration   allusion   anthropomorphism   cliché   connotation   denotation   dialect   dialogue   euphemism   flashback   foreshadow   hyperbole   idiom imagery   irony   litote   metaphor   metonymy   onomatopoeia   personification   portmanteay words   proverb   pun   sarcasm   simile   symbolism   understatement

---

Elements of Literature

allusion   antagonist   author   biography   character   characterization   cliffhanger   climax   conflict   dialect   dialogue   drama   epilogue   exposition   fantasy   mood   narrator   novel   plot   point of view   protagonist   resolution   satire   science fiction   setting   stereotype   style   suspense   symbol   theme   tone   traits

---

Poetry

acrostic　alliteration　assonance　ballad　cinquain　clerihew　consonance
couplet　enjambment　epic　epitaph　foot　haiku　imagery　limerick　line
lyric　meter　ode　onomatopoeia　poet　poetry　quatrain　rhythm　rhyme
scansion　sonnet　stanza　syllables　tanka　tercet　verse　villanelle

Famous Authors and Their Works

Alcott　[Van] Allsburg　Anderson　Austen　Blume　Carle　Christie　Cleary
Dahl　Dickens　Gaiman　Grahame　Irving　L'Engle　Lee　Lewis　Lowry
Milne　Paterson　Poe　Potter　Rey　Riordan　Rowling　Sachar
Sendak　Shakespeare　Shelley　Stevenson　Tolkien　Twain　White

Words, Roots, and Affixes

acrimonious　affix　amic　ant　algia　antitoxin　bellicose　bene
chronology　cide　clarify　contradict　decade　destruction　dorm　empathy
immortal　incorporate　incredible　ingratitude　invincible　involuntary
juvenile　microscope　pend　prefix　root　senile　sequel　solitary
suffix　sume　tang　temporary　telescope

Vocabulary

abode　acknowledge　affliction　bestow　brawl　candid　casualty　confront
corrupt　covet　despondent　docile　enthrall　feud　firebrand　fruitless
gravity　grim　headlong　implore　insinuate　intensify　magnitude
maternal　prowess　unscathed　uncanny　vista　whim　wince

More Vocabulary

acclaim　acrid　apathy　bellow　bewilder　braggart　browse
canine　capsize　clamber　customary　dismal　distraught　erode
figment　flabbergast　flaw　gratify　gruesome　inundate　loath
mirth　narrative　nimble　nomadic　reprimand　rupture
subtle　sullen　toxic　utmost　vicious　wary　wrath

Synonyms and Antonyms

abate　accelerate　agitate　antagonize　aspire　authentic　avert　beseech
astute　bigoted　blatant　capricious　concur　debut　dumbfound　exuberant
fathom　flagrant　law　gaudy　grimy　impede　infamous　infuriate
legitimate　lethal　mortify　negligent　noteworthy　perturbed　pluck
ponder　robust　substantial　trickle　vindictive